Get Out of Your Way™

The Step By Step Guide For Entrepreneurs
to Attract, Recruit & Retain A Winning Team

Wendy Sneddon

Published by
10-10-10 Publishing
Markham, Ontario
CANADA

ISBN 9781532899409

For information about special discounts for bulk purchases, please
contact 10-10-10 Publishing at 1-888-504-6257

Contents

Appendices

Testimonials

I have known Wendy working in several management and consultancy roles. She has experienced many of the challenges that entrepreneurs face, and her insights into how to make businesses flourish, especially in relation to the all important people aspects will be invaluable.

Mark Johnston MA VetMB PhD MRCVS, Managing Director, Vetstream Ltd

Wendy is someone with a big vision and a very practical attitude. She has experience in many areas as well as her own personal awareness of what it takes to run a business successfully, so she speaks from the heart and the head, and that's a winning combination. This book takes a simple and pragmatic approach, step-by-step, to help entrepreneurs figure out how to prioritise and manage their time so that they can work on the business, as well as in the business.

Georgia Parker, Cascade Coaching & Training

Foreword

Have you ever thought about your life purpose? Like most people, you probably have not. Have you ever thought that it was time to transform your life, but never knew how? You probably have lots of things you love doing many things you want to experience and goals you want to achieve, and you dream of an extraordinary life. Again, if you are like most people, your life is filled with activities, obligations and commitments that have nothing to do with your goals or your dreams. You may be spending your life running faster and faster, trying to keep up, and at the same time falling further and further away from living that extraordinary life about which you are dreaming.

By building a team of people within your business who are as passionate about what they do as you are, by selecting those who share the same values and beliefs, you will create an awesome working environment, your business will thrive and you will be able to live your life's purpose.

I am impressed with Wendy's passion for her subject. I know from experience that finding and keeping great people can be a challenge! I recommend this as a must read for entrepreneurs who are growing their business and building their teams. Getting the foundations for your business laid down is crucial, and this will help you in all aspects of your business, not just in retaining great people.

In this book you will find very simple ideas, guidelines and suggestions that you can follow to empower you to transform your business culture, and have lots of business success. Start applying this now and move towards becoming an extraordinary business to work for. I'm sure there are many ideas and suggestions in this book that will resonate with you.

Raymond Aaron
NY Times Bestselling Author

To my husband William,
my daughter Charlotte & my son Cameron
I want to thank you for your patience and unwavering support
in all that I do!

Acknowledgements

I want to thank all of those great entrepreneurs I have been fortunate enough to work closely with over the years, who gave me inspiration for this book.

Thank you to Rachel Johnsen, the best flatmate ever, for her support and her inspiration.

Thank you, Lynn Ballantyne Wardlaw, for your critical eye, helping me to perfect my masterpiece.

My thanks also go to the many business owners who over the years have complained about the lack of great people to fill their positions, without taking any responsibility for what they might have done differently.

A huge thank you to my fellow "Awesome Authors" for all their support and encouragement to get it done.

More importantly, I thank Mr. Raymond Aaron, NY Times Top 10 Bestselling Author, and Naval Kumar, my personal mentor and coach, and their team for assisting me with my book.

Inspiration from the Author

I have worked with many small business owners over the years. Of all the tough challenges they face, there is one common struggle – managing people! I have heard it said that people leave managers, not companies. I have also found this to be very true. All too often managers are put in positions of responsibility by default rather than being selected for their aptitude. This can work, providing the new manager is offered training and support to make the transition, however, more often than not, there is little support – and so the challenges begin.

This is often true of entrepreneurs. They have great ideas, the drive and passion to get things done and succeed, but they lack the skills in leading a team. The business evolves around them, with little or no consideration for organisational development. Entrepreneurs who have taken that leap into self-employment, either because they came up with an amazing idea or because they are fabulous at what they do, have to make the transition into leaders – often without knowing or really understanding what that means. This is of course a sweeping generalisation, there are many who are natural born leaders!

"You can't expect employees to exceed your customer's expectations if you don't exceed your employees' expectations of management."
Howard Schultz, Founder of Starbucks

Leadership and management are disciplines in themselves; take your management role seriously! There is a lot of information to learn if you want to get it right and build a successful, high performing team.

Research shows that business success comes down to motivated, engaged teams. There are lots of initiatives to help you to identify how engaged your teams are, and these will provide great feedback for you to build a strategy to improve employee engagement.

It all starts with recruiting the right people for your team.

This book has been written for entrepreneurs who are recruiting their first employee and building their first team. It is ideal for small business owners who can't afford to employ a HR support, and will help you to set up a basic system to attract, recruit and retain great people within your business. These simple steps will ensure you have the correct procedures in place, which, if followed, will help you successfully recruit a winning team.

It will also help those business owners who are struggling to retain good people, by giving them a framework to review their current foundations and to identify where they need strengthening.

By the time you have read this book you will understand what foundations you need to have in place to build great teams. You will know what systems you require to recruit and select great people, and how to keep them!

Chapter 1
Your First Time?

So, you're an entrepreneur. Congratulations! You have started up a business, things are going great, you're doing really well, sales are good, but you are working 20 hours a day, 7 days a week!

You are exhausted! You hardly see your family or friends, and you have no social life. Life can't go on like this – you will burn out!

So it's time to bring someone in to assist you in continuing the success.

I know what you are thinking: "no-one can do what you do", right?

Wrong!

You've been covering all the roles in business, and now it's time to bring in the experts who are going to help you take your business to the next level. It is so important to take the time to consider what skills you have, where your strengths lie, and where your weaknesses are. The table in Appendix 1 shows the roles and levels required within a business. Put your name in the boxes where your strengths lie, and what's left are the gaps you need to fill.

Below are the main roles that are required to run a successful business:

HR: All businesses are about people and the relationships they build with the team and with customers and the service they deliver. There are legal requirements to comply with, such as having contracts in place and a handbook stating their rights as an employee. More importantly, how are you going to attract them and what are you offering? – I don't just mean pay. People are looking for a better work-life balance. What is it really like to work with you? What will people learn and what are the opportunities? How can you get them excited about being part of your journey?

Finance: Knowing your numbers is key to business success. Have some key performance indicators that will help you to monitor performance; check these daily and stay close to them so you can act quickly if your business performance starts to drift.

Operations: How does it work on a day-to-day basis? Write an operations manual that sets out what you want to achieve and how you want to achieve it.

Marketing: How are you getting your product and/or service out there? What kind of budget do you have? You should be spending at least 5% of your turnover on marketing activities.

IT: All businesses require some form of IT infrastructure. It is advantageous to seek advice in the early days. Consider what you might need over the next 5 to 10 years and invest in equipment and software than can grow and expand with you.

There are also three levels of responsibility for each role within a business:
- Strategic – responsible for planning the long term strategy of the business
- Management – put the strategy into place at the right time and make it happen
- Day to day – getting the work done

See appendix 1 Organisation Planning Template

Up until now it's been just you, filling all of these roles. Now it's time to delegate some of these responsibilities to more appropriate people.

You have some choices; you can outsource some, or all, of these roles, or you can recruit your own team. It's time to get out of your way and let the experts in to do their thing!

Once you have made the decision – and it is probably one of the most important decisions you will ever make – you have a long way to go until you are ready to hire. There are several things you need to consider and have in place to help your new team understand what you are all about, what you want to achieve and how you expect them to behave.

The elements required to build the foundations of a successful business:

Element	Description
Vision	Your destination. The future you want to create.
Mission	What you have to do to get to your destination.
Values	How you keep on track.
Strategy	Your plan of action for the journey.
Tactics	How you allocate resources.
Goals	What you want to achieve.

From the Barrett Values Centre https://www.valuescentre.com /mapping-values/culture/culture-strategy

Vision:
You need to have a clear vision for the future, "the WHAT"– so people know where you are taking the business. What are your ambitions for growth, what do you want to achieve, what do you want to be known for?

Mission:
You need to have a mission statement that easily sums up what your

business does. It's the phrase that describes HOW you are going to achieve your vision!

Values:
What is important to you and to your business? Your values form the basis of your culture and become the principles you live and breathe by.

Culture:
The Culture is about what it is like to work in your business. How do you want people to work and play? What kind of culture do you want to develop? How do you want people to behave? What type of people do you want to associate with?

Once you are clear about what you want from these areas in your business, you can go on to create your job descriptions and person specifications. This will help you to:

- clarify what type of person and what skills and experience you are looking for
- create the perfect advert to attract them
- obtain the criteria to design your interview
- make your final decision

The secret to success in business lies with the experience, drive and ambition of the manager. Select managers who believe in your vision, mission, values and cultures. You need them to back your beliefs, share out responsibilities and foster team engagement. Invest in training for your managers in how to support your team, and your business will thrive.

See what happens when you "act as if" this is true...
"Behind every behaviour is a positive intention"
from the Pre suppositions of NLP
(http://www.anlp.org/presuppositions-of-nlp)

Hold this belief and you will view situations differently. You are likely to become less judgemental and listen to every side of the story. You are likely to be more open to giving people a second chance.

Behave with integrity – if this is what you expect from your team – and make sure you are setting the example, and do what you say you are going to do.

HMRC:
If you haven't already done so, you also need to register as an employer with HMRC. You can do it online. https://www.gov.uk /register-employer

Chapter 2
Developing Your Vision and Mission

What do I mean by Vision?

"Begin with the end in mind."
Stephen Covey, *7 Habits of Highly Effective People*

The vision is an inspirational and compelling story about the future you want to create for you and your business. It is about where you want to take your business, the dreams and ambitions that you have, and what you want to achieve. What do you want to be remembered for? Just as Stephen Covey describes in his famous book about the seven habits of highly effective people, the very first habit is "begin with the end in mind."

What is your exit strategy for your business? Are you retiring and passing it on to a family member? Are you creating something of value that you want to sell? Who is your ideal buyer? Consider this now, as you may want to grow and develop into a business that will be of interest to that particular company or person in the future.

When you think about what you want your life to be like in the future, consider how much money you want to make. What turnover do you want to achieve? Who will be your ideal customers? What other products might you want to develop in the future? What other ideas do you have that will take you forward to help you achieve your end goal?

How to write your Vision

What is your destination? What future are you creating? What do you want to be known for?

Describe what you deliver – not what you do. So if you make socks, you are keeping feet warm and cosy.

What is unique about you? Why should people buy your socks instead of your competitors' socks?

What accolades have you achieved or do you want to achieve in the future – are there any specific to your industry?

What are your financial goals?

What do I mean by Mission?

Your mission statement describes how you are going to achieve your vision. It defines in a paragraph or so, a business's reason for existence. It embodies its philosophies, goals, ambitions and more. A business that attempts to operate without a mission statement runs the risk of missing out on customers and employees as they don't know what you are about.

Some examples of mission statements are:

Ford Motor Company: "We are a global family with a proud heritage passionately committed to providing personal mobility for people around the world."

Nike: "To bring inspiration and innovation to every athlete in the world."

American Express: "At American Express, we have the mission to be the world's most respected service brand. To do this we have established a culture that supports our team members so they can provide exceptional service to our customers."

Ikea: "At Ikea our mission is to create a better everyday life for many people. Our business idea supports this by offering a wide range of well-designed functional home furnishing products at prices so low that as many people as possible will be able to afford them."

Universal Health Services, Inc: "Our mission is to provide superior quality healthcare services that: patients recommend to family and friends, physicians prefer for their patients, purchasers select for their clients, employees are proud of, and investors seek for long term returns."

How to write your mission statement

So what do you do? Sum it up as succinctly as possible. Who benefits from what you do and in what way? A mission statement is a short statement, around 15 words, that sums up three basic things:

1. What you do;
2. Who you do it for; and
3. Under what conditions

Ensure that you have integrity when writing this – don't make claims you can't substantiate! Saying you are the best vet in the UK is too general a statement, and unless you have an award that says so, it's false. Your team won't feel it and your clients won't believe you.

How are your vision and missions statement relevant when hiring?

Jobseekers want to know that your business has an identity and they want to know what you stand for. If you want to keep a team motivated, the mission statement will give them your direction and inspiration.

Take action...
Create your vision and design a mission statement so everyone knows what you want to achieve and how you are going to get there.

Be clear about what you need.

What is your vision for your business? Where do you see yourself in 5 and 10 years?

_____

_____

_____

_____

_____

_____

What is your mission statement? What do you do, who do you do it for and under what conditions?

_____

_____

_____

_____

_____

_____

_____

Chapter 3
Developing Your Values and Culture

"When your values are clear to you,
making decisions becomes easier."
Roy E Disney

All too often the values that make up the culture of a business either reflect the underlying beliefs and values of the current leaders, or they reflect the values of past leaders.

Most businesses don't pay attention to the culture, so the values and beliefs of the leaders become "the way we do things here".

When there is no alignment between the values of the culture of the business and the personal values of the employees, the result is low performance, low levels of staff engagement and poor quality of products and services. This has a significant impact on the financial performance of the business.

When the values of the business are in alignment with the values of the employees, the result is high performance, a high level of team engagement, and a drive for excellence with the quality of products and services.

When the values of the business and the team are united, the culture of a business is able to attract and retain talented individuals. This will give business a significant commercial advantage, especially when great people are in short supply. Having your values integrated into your business culture also helps you to build a strong brand. Brand values and company values are like two sides of the same coin.

The success of a business is directly related to the degree of coordination between the underlying values of the leaders and the values of the team. Long-term, sustainable success is dependent on the culture that the leaders create.

The culture that leaders create is dependent on the behaviours of the leaders and their relationships to other leaders and their relationships with their teams. Leaders whose energies are about status seeking, empire-building, and internal competition create toxic environments.

Business transformation begins with the personal transformation of the leaders. The key
to developing a high-performance culture lies with the leadership.

In order to grasp the process and benefits of a whole-system approach to developing your culture, it is important to measure the desired cultures of a successful business, thereby identifying the desired leadership styles. For cultural alignment, it is necessary to have a clear understanding of where you want your business to go.

What do I mean by Values?

Values are the things that you believe are important to you in life and work.

They will determine your priorities, and, deep down, they're probably the measures you use to tell if your life is turning out the way you want it to.

When the things you do and how you behave match your values, life is usually good – you're satisfied and content. But when these don't align with your personal values, that's when things feel wrong. This can be a real source of unhappiness.

This is why making a conscious effort to identify your values is so important.

A-Z of Values

Accountability	Honesty
Achievement	Humour/fun
Balance (home/work)	Independence
Commitment	Integrity
Compassion	Initiative
Competence	Intuition
Continuous learning	Making a difference
Cooperation	Open communication
Courage	Openness
Creativity	Personal Fulfilment
Enthusiasm	Personal growth
Efficiency	Power
Ethics	Respect
Excellence	Responsibility
Fairness	Risk-taking
Family	Self-discipline
Financial gain	Success
Friendships	Trust
Future generations	Wisdom
Health	

How to elicit your Values

Check out the list of examples of values above. These are words and statements that mean something to us. Select 5 values, either from the list above or come up with your own, and write them in the table in Appendix 2.

Richard Barrett set up the Barrett Values Centre and has developed a number of Cultural Transformation Tools. They do a great free personal values assessment: https://survey.valuescentre.com /survey.html?id=s1TAEQUStmzOG_33NjatBw&locale=en

What do I mean by Culture?

Your culture is the ethos of your business. Be clear about who you are and what you stand for. Defining your culture is going to help you to develop a competitive advantage. Ethical values and strong employee engagement are just as important as the quality of the products and services that you sell.

A failure to embrace values, culture and ethical leadership has led to the demise of many of the larger corporations over the past few decades. Consider the failures at Enron, Northern Rock, and RBS. They are testimony to this fact; billions of dollars of shareholder value and employee pensions were wiped out overnight because of the actions of a leadership team who were only out for themselves.

How do you create the ideal Culture?

How do you behave when you are at work? Do you greet everyone with a cheery "good morning?" Do you check in with the team to see how everyone is? This makes everyone feel welcome and feel comfortable. Or are you a "mood hoover?" Do you suck the life out of everyone when you walk into a room? It is up to you to set the example of how you want your team to behave at work.

How do you want your team members to feel when they are at work?

How do you want them to behave and interact with each other?

Produce a statement that describes your culture – expand on your mission statement and elaborate on what type of relationships and behaviours you expect from your team to help them achieve this.

Once you have decided on the type of culture you want to develop, as a business leader it is your responsibility to ensure that the culture is disseminated throughout your team, you need to be prepared to live and breathe it, leading by example. Day in and day out, you need to ensure that your team believes in it, and reinforce, recognise and reward behaviour that is consistent with your culture.

Here are some tips to help you create the ideal culture to foster employee engagement and business success:

1. Employ the right people first time round
Employ people for their passion and commitment first, experience second, and credentials third. Anyone can write an impressive CV, so look for people who are interested in the same things as you are. Ask the questions: What do you love about your career? What inspires you? What courses in school did you dread? You want to get a sense of what the potential employee believes in.

2. Have a consistent communication strategy
Once you have the right people, they need feedback! Sit down regularly with them and discuss what is going well and what isn't. Celebrate successes and analyse failures. A strong growth culture is one that recognises when things don't work and adjusts to rectify the problems. Your team needs to feel safe and trusted. They should understand that they can speak freely without fear of repercussion.

Great cultures grow around people who listen to each other, to clients and to stakeholders. It's also important to listen to what's happening in your market. What developments and trends are happening?

3. Weed out the "victims"
A team of passionate people can be easily compromised by the wrong people. One of the most destructive corporate weeds is the victim. Victims are the ones who complain about everything, taking no responsibility, sowing doubt, and stifling passion. Maybe these people simply aren't a good fit. Your passion isn't theirs. Constructive criticism is healthy, but relentless complaining is toxic to your team and your business. Identify quickly who these people are and replace them!

4. Work hard, play hard
Passionate teams require a strong work ethic. It's easy to do what you love. These days, not many industries these days thrive on a forty-hour work week. A culture where everyone understands that long hours are sometimes required will work if this sacrifice is recognised and rewarded.

5. Be clear about your ambitions
Ambition is sometimes seen as a negative these days, but without it we would stagnate. You need a culture that supports big steps and powerful beliefs. More importantly share them and create a compelling vision for your team to aspire to.

6. Celebrate differences
When choosing students for a program/degree course, most universities now consider more than just marks. If you had a dozen straight-A students who were from the same socio-economic background and the same geographical area, you might not get much in the way of interesting debate or interaction. Great cultures are built on a diversity of background, experience and interests. These differences generate energy, which is critical to any enterprise.

7. Create the space

Now, innovation is prized. When designing your workspace, promote as much team interaction as possible. Design spaces where the team will come together, both in workspace and in common rest areas. It is this interaction of the team at all levels that helps to breed revolutionary ideas. Foster creative chats over coffee, or create lunch and learn sessions to share knowledge and generate discussions. Do you provide opportunity for this? – is there some way you can?

8. Take the long view

If your business is dependent on this quarter's sales or this month's targets, then it is handicapped by short-term thinking. Passionate leaders take the long view. The culture needs to look ahead, not just in months but in years and even decades.

How is culture relevant when hiring?

In today's climate where unemployment is low, there are many more jobs than applicants. According to the latest Office for National Statistics, unemployment fell by 102,000 to 1.86 million in the three months to the end of January 2016. The employment rate is at 73.3%, the highest rate of people in work since 1971!

Jobseekers have the luxury of choosing from a variety of positions. You will find that you have to really sell your business and your team and clearly state why people would want to work for you.

Employees want to have clear expectations set for them. They want regular feedback so that they know when they are doing a good job. They want to have fun at work with colleagues who are respectful to one another. Consider your business; what have you got to offer?

Be open about having an open, friendly, respectful culture, and you will attract the right people to your team.

All too often I hear employers complain about the lack of good applicants, about how they spend time and money training them up and they leave.

Employees are no longer prepared to work long hours for little or no recognition. This generation is focused on work-life balance. They want to come to work and enjoy it, knowing what is expected of them and be recognised and rewarded appropriately. They want a shift pattern that gives them time with their families, and to take up hobbies. I know businesses who are still not issuing contracts or preparing job descriptions. Is it any wonder why some people don't perform? They don't really know what's expected of them!

It is time for you as an employer to take responsibility for this. Carry out an exit interview. Why are they leaving? What could you have done differently for them that would have enabled them to stay?

Take action now...

Agree on a set of values for your business and clearly describe how they integrate into your culture.

What are your values? What's important to you and to your business?

_____

_____

_____

_____

_____

What's your culture like? How do you want people to feel when they work for you?

_____

_____

_____

_____

_____

_____

_____

Chapter 4
How to Define WHAT You Need in Your Team

Over the years I have worked with a number of businesses to assist with recruitment. What many of them have in common is that they were not clear about what kind of person they were looking for. Can you say that you know exactly what you are looking for? If not, how can you be confident that you are taking on the right person for the job? How often have you gone through a lengthy recruitment process and then ended up with the wrong person? Have you been frustrated with the time, money and resources that have been wasted in making the wrong decision? Or have they not stayed with you because after a while they realised you have no foundations in place, or they don't share your values?

You need to establish a policy for recruitment. The recruitment and selection decision is one of the most important decisions you will make, and getting it right will contribute significantly towards your effectiveness as a business. The recruitment and selection process will set out how you want your business to recruit people and will ensure that you select new recruits who share your values and understand your culture.

The recruitment policy ensures your recruitment and selection process will:
* be fair and consistent
* be non-discriminatory
* conform to statutory regulations and agreed best practice
* be compliant with the Equality Act 2010

- be designed to attract the best possible applicants for vacancies
- ensure that all applicants are treated fairly and without discrimination

The procedures set out in your recruitment and selection policy should be followed each and every time a new team member is recruited at any level, from a receptionist or administrator to an office manager or company director.

The recruitment and selection policy should clearly set out procedures for:
- the recruitment process as a whole
- advertising of vacancies
- recruitment materials
- the candidate application process
- short-listing
- interview procedures
- offer/rejection process
- referencing

The policy should include your policy on equal opportunities – a statement declaring that you will hire employees based on their ability to do the job and not discriminate in any way. Outline your recruitment process. List your job descriptions, person specifications and any other job information. Consider your advertising policy – where you will advertise? Ensure you comply with your equal opportunities statement. What is your selection process? How will you make your decisions and what information will you collect? Application forms, CVs, psychometric tests, references, interviews, work based assessments?

Carry out exit interviews – follow up with leavers, get feedback to help you identify issues and further improve the workplace.

SAMPLE RECRUITMENT AND SELECTION POLICY

POLICY
The purpose of this recruitment policy is to enable the selection of the best person for the job, using a structured approach to the recruitment process. It ensures that consistency and fairness is achieved and complies with our own equal opportunities policy and with current employment legislation. All job applicants will be treated equally, irrespective of their sex, marital status, race, ethnic origin, disability, religion, creed, sexual orientation, age or political views.

The recruitment and selection decision is one of the most important, and getting it right will contribute significantly towards our effectiveness as a business. The recruitment and selection procedure will help us to ensure that we select new recruits who share our values and show a willingness to learn, adapt and work as part of a team.

This policy ensures our recruitment and selection process will :
- be fair and consistent
- be non-discriminatory
- conform to all statutory regulations and agreed best practice

Equal Opportunities

The company seeks to recruit employees on the basis of their ability and the requirements of the post.

We will ensure that no applicant receives less favorable treatment than another on the grounds of disability, gender, race, religion or belief, age, sexual orientation, marital status, parental status, caring responsibilities or hours of work.

To ensure that these policy aims are achieved, all managers will receive training in effective recruitment and selection.

The Recruitment Process

The following procedure will be used when a post is to be filled:

Define the job. Draw up a job description and consider the salary and benefits you will offer.

Prepare a person specification. Describe the type of person you are looking for to fill this post.

Collate information appropriate for the post, ready for emailing out to potential candidates. This should include:
- job description and if appropriate, the person specification
- information on <company name>
- terms and conditions of employment, including salary and benefits

It is important that this pack (information) is carefully put together in order to present a professional image of the company.

Choose an option for selecting suitable permanent candidates:
- internal advert within the business
- check through previous applications
- external advert within the job centre
- external advert in the local press
- external advert in the national press
- external advert in the appropriate technical/professional journal
- recruitment agency
- external advert on relevant job sites
- social media (eg Linkedin, Twitter, Facebook)

Design the advert. All adverts must contain as much information as possible to ensure the correct recruitment group is targeted and reduce unsuitable applications, while remaining cost-effective.

The Selection Process

Appropriate selection procedures must be used for each post. Procedures may vary. At its simplest, this may involve a straight forward interview and skills testing. For more senior posts, psychometric testing, presentations to the interview panel on a chosen topic and/or a series of individual interviews on various topics may be included.

The application forms received by the closing date must be shortlisted against the person specification. Design a screening matrix to assist with this process which will provide a record of the reasons why an applicant is, or is not, shortlisted, as well as making it easier to select the right candidates to be shortlisted.

Invite the shortlisted candidates for an interview; candidates who have not been shortlisted should also be informed.

At least two people should be involved on the interview panel. Prior to the interview, each panellist will receive an interview pack containing:
- copies of application forms / cv's
- blank interview questionnaires
- a copy of the job advertisement
- a copy of the job description
- a copy of the person specification

At the interview, the appointing manager will:
- decide on the interview format
- determine which areas to concentrate on with the questioning
- decide on who will chair the interview panel
- ensure that the interview questionnaire is completed as fully as possible
- ensure that equal opportunities legislation is strictly adhered to, with no discrimination shown on any grounds.

When all candidates have been interviewed, the panel will score them appropriately using a Candidate Assessment form and based on this decide on the most suitable person for the post The unsuccessful candidates should also be informed of the panel's decision. It may be appropriate to wait until the successful candidate has accepted the position before doing this. The appointing manager will:

- arrange to inform the successful candidate as soon as possible, agree on a start date and starting salary, subject to satisfactory references
- write to the appointee, offering the post (providing satisfactory references and pre-employment checks have been received)
- contact all unsuccessful candidates with outcome of interview
- initiate a personnel file and computer entry for the new team member
- deal with any requirements for relocation expenses or the finding of temporary accommodation for the appointee
- obtain references
- arrange pre-employment checks as appropriate
- arrange an individual programme of induction for the new start's first week of employment

Exit Interviews

All employees who leave the employment of the company voluntarily will have an exit interview with their manager before their last day of employment.

Exit interviews provide the opportunity for departing employees to discuss their reasons for leaving. The information provided is useful in identifying trends, learning and development, and evaluating the effectiveness of HR policies and practices.

The appropriate line manager should receive all appropriate information, such as recommendations made for change, or significant issues raised in the questionnaire, whilst bearing in mind confidentiality issues. The exit interview questionnaire will be retained on the employee's personal file.

Job Description

Before you advertise for a position, review the job description and ensure it is relevant to the job and completely up to date.

As any business evolves, so do the day to day duties and responsibilities involved within roles. Take the time to ensure that if you are replacing someone, the job description is correct and fully up to date. This will save you time, resources and money in the future by helping to ensure that you are recruiting the right person for the right role. If the job description isn't accurate, and you take on a new person, you will be risking a high turnover rate as their expectations may well differ to the realities of the day-to-day aspects of the role.

Developing a job description for each role is essential to the success of your business. They create clarity for both the employee and you as their manager. According to Gallup, one of the biggest motivating factors for employees is clarity within their role. That is, they know what they're supposed to do and how to do it. Your expectations of them are clearly laid out so there is no dispute over what they should or shouldn't be doing.

A job description is a written statement explaining:
- job title, hours of work, place of work, who to report to
- why the role exists
- what roles and responsibilities the job holder will have
- what specific tasks they are required to do

Why have job descriptions?

Job descriptions will improve your ability to manage your team. They will:

- clarify expectations
- enable you to measure performance
- provide a clear description of the job
- help with structuring fair pay and grading systems
- provide a reference tool in case of a dispute or for discipline issues
- highlight areas for training and development
- provide an objective reference point for performance reviews

The job description should be used during the recruitment process so the applicants understand the role and what is required of them, ensuring the person you select can fully commit to the job.

Roles & Responsibilities

The first paragraph of any job description is perhaps the most important part – it is where you capture the attention of the applicant and hopefully make them want to read on and submit an application.

This is very much a summary of the position. When defining the main duties and responsibilities within a role, make sure you are presenting the day-to-day duties, expectations and results, in a clear and concise manner.
- What areas of the business will they be responsible for?
- What will they do on a day-to-day basis?

Use bullet points and list all aspects of the role, not just the desirable tasks; also include the more mundane, although it is always a clever idea to mix these up to keep the role interesting. As a rule, the first and last bullet points are the ones you really want to be noticed, so the more mundane tasks can be inserted in the middle.

Consider your applicants; junior or apprentice posts will need very specific descriptions of the day-to-day tasks. For more senior managerial or technical positions, also include what key performance indicators you want to measure.

In my experience, employers often don't consider what experience and/or qualifications they are looking for in their new recruit. You MUST decide this from the offset and make it very clear in the job description.

How much previous experience do you require them to have, and why? What qualifications do they need to have in order to do the job? You should also bear in mind that you may have to demonstrate the necessity of any experience or qualifications you specify, otherwise you may fall foul of age discrimination legislation. For example, if you specify 3 years' experience in a particular role, you are excluding applicants under a certain age. Think about why you think the role requires this level of experience. Equally, you may see a role as requiring somebody who is willing to train and take qualifications to go further in your company; however, you should not specify "recent graduate" or "school leaver" as this would be discriminatory.

You want team members who have a flexible attitude and approach to the workplace, employees who will embrace change. In the early days, your business will experience lots of change as you grow and develop into your vision.

See Appendix 3 for a job description template.

Chapter 5
How to Define WHO You Need

The Person Specification

It doesn't need to be said that recruitment is all about finding the right person for the job. So, do you know exactly what you are looking for in that person?

A person specification is crucial, as it describes exactly that.

Employers will use the person specification to define exactly what they are looking for.

It is important to consider your requirements in all areas, including qualifications, professional experience, skills and knowledge, and perhaps most importantly, personal qualities – you want to ensure that any new recruit will fit in with your existing team.

Be realistic in what you are looking for. Carefully consider what are your absolute minimum requirements for the role? What skills would purely be an added bonus. You don't want to rule people out before they've even applied based on a lack of skills that are not essential for them to do a good job, or a lack of skills that you can easily teach them if they were to be successful. After all, you'll be hoping that all applicants demonstrate a desire to further develop their skills.

- Skills
  - what's essential
  - what's desirable

- Qualifications
  - what's essential
  - what's desirable
- Behaviours
  - what's essential
  - what's desirable

Be clear about WHO you are looking for

What type of person are you looking for? What type and level of experience do you want them to have? What skills and behaviours do you want them to have?

See appendix 4 for a template person specification

Chapter 6
Writing a Compelling Advert

Any advert that you post will essentially be the first impression that the applicant has of your business, and you need this to be positive in order to ensure that you are not creating barriers for potential applicants.

You must ensure that the advert contains sufficient and accurate information relating to the role by following the guidelines for the job description and person specification, and ensure that the advert is visually appealing by following some simple processes.

Once the advert is complete, proof read it and get someone else to read it too – they'll be able to tell you if it's appealing or if it doesn't hold their attention.

It goes without saying that you need to ensure your adverts are consistent in terms of their format and branding so that applicants become familiar with your business as you recruit over the years.

You should therefore have developed a corporate template which incorporates the company logo, colours, typeface and so on. You can do this in-house on a decent word processor, or have it designed professionally by an agency.

Once you have a look you are happy with, all you need is the content!

Where do you advertise?
Professional journals?
What social media will they interact with?

What online sites will they use?
What agencies could you use?

There are a number of forums in which you can advertise your vacancy, but the key is finding the ones that work best for you and have a better chance of reaching the applicants that you are trying to attract.

There are many ways to advertise free of charge, and it is always essential to advertise your vacancies internally to existing staff and to advertise on your own website.

Contact any previous applicants that have given you their permission to keep their details on file.

Some membership websites offer a forum to advertise vacancies online too – make full use of this service and get the most out of your membership!

When paying to advertise your vacancy, be mindful of your budget – you want to ensure that you will be getting the right applicants through. Keep a record of the applicants that come through from each area, and the relevance of each application, so that you can monitor if these means are cost effective for future recruitment campaigns.

About your company

Come up with a headline to attract attention to your advert. The job title itself is surprisingly important, and you should think carefully about what you call the job. Studies have shown that the job title is more important than salary to potential applicants! The top of the advert should contain the job title and the location of the vacancy.

This is your opportunity to really *sell* your business to prospective applicants. Focus on the successes your business has had, and your vision for the future. Highlight what makes you unique and potentially attractive to applicants. How do you differentiate yourself from your competition? Really sell your business!

Describe the details of the job so potential applicants know what they would be applying for. Communicate your *unique selling point*. What is it that makes this job better, or different from other similar jobs, to attract to potential applicants.

Take a look at your competitors' adverts – what stands out? What can you say to make yours stand out more?

What are you offering?

What is the package? This is not just about money. What will they experience during their time with you? What are you like to work for? What is your culture, your values? Job seekers are interviewing you! They will research your business, and they will ask people who know you what you are like. How will you stand out from similar types of businesses so that the applicant chooses you?

Always indicate the salary range and other benefits on offer. Where salaries are competitive, additional benefits can make or break an applicant's decision. Include as much information as possible, but don't promise anything that you are unable to deliver.

If you want to wait and see who applies before committing to a salary level, then you need to ensure that an appropriate message about the benefits package is given out. For example, the salary is highly competitive and will depend on experience and qualifications.

How do you want them to apply?

Consider how you want the individual to apply, whether it's a standard application form (which is great for the comparison of a large number of applicants) or a CV (which is good for more senior jobs as it gives the applicant a better chance to express themselves).

Provide your phone number so that prospective applicants can contact you to discuss the detail of the job if necessary.

It is also good practice to put a closing date in your advert, with realistic timescales for responding.

Job adverts don't just reach potential applicants. A job advert is a message to your competitors and the wider business community that you're hiring, so always bear this in mind when constructing the advert.

See Appendix 5 for an advert template.
See Appendix 6 for an example application form.

Chapter 7
Interview & Selection

"Hiring people is an art, not a science, and CVs can't tell you if someone will fit into your company's culture." Howard Shultz, founder of Starbucks.

When you are inundated with applications, you need a way of screening out the best candidates to interview, see who is the best fit, on paper – that's when you need a standardised screening process.

In order to set up interviews and select the right person for the job, you need to get a few things organised. So, you have placed your advert and have had a number of CVs and application forms through. Have a transparent process for deciding whom to put through to interview and objective reasons for not putting through the rest. Applicants can challenge you if they believe you have been discriminatory in any way, even at this stage of the recruitment process.

Screening Applications

After your agreed closing date, gather up your CVs and/or applications forms. Design an applicant screening matrix to record that you have gone through each applicant, looking for the same criteria.

Make a list of the qualifications, skills and experience that you mentioned in your job advert so you can tick off what they do or don't have. Depending on the position, you may also have some essential criteria to include from your person specification list.

Go through each application and tick off from your list what qualifications, skills and experience they have mentioned. Have they provided the information you asked for in their covering letter? I would disregard any application where the applicant hasn't bothered to take the time to introduce him or herself, or explain what would make them a great candidate for the job.

If attention to detail is important to the job, how has their CV and application form been presented? Are there spelling errors or inconsistencies?

See appendix 7 for an example of an applicant screening form.

Selecting applicants to interview

You have screened your applications, so each applicant will now have a score. The applicants you put forward for interview should be the best fit, on paper; now you need to meet them and find out if they are the right fit for your culture. There may be times when an applicant doesn't score highly enough to warrant an interview on your matrix, but there is something about their application that has grabbed your attention, and you think they're worth meeting. Don't ignore your gut feeling. Invite them for an interview anyway. Remember, you are looking for someone to become part of your team, and you want to see what he or she is really like. Plan an interview that will help you see the candidates at their very best.

Preparing for interviews

What is your plan for the interviews? How are you going to discover if the applicants whose CVs suggested they were a good match, actually are? What are your options?
- Telephone interviews
- Face to face interviews
- Video/Skype interviews

- Panel interviews (presentations)
- Work trials/placement

Telephone interviews: Set up a mutually convenient time, advise the candidate how much time you expect to take and ask them to take the call somewhere they won't be interrupted. Prepare the candidate to answer a mixture of competency based questions and behavioural questions by phone. This is great if you are interviewing for a receptionist or a call centre position where telephone manner is very important. Have a checklist ready to ensure you cover everything.

Face to face interviews: Hold the interviews onsite if you can; it always helps if the candidates can see where they will be working. Find a quiet space where you won't be interrupted. Make the candidate feel as relaxed as possible and keep the conversation informal. Generally, I offer them a cup of tea, and I will talk initially about the business and the team. This gives them a chance to relax and calm down. I will then ask them to tell me about themselves and what brought them here today. Once everyone is more comfortable I will start on the more thought provoking and experiential questions, as well as questions that will take more consideration.

It is useful to help prepare the candidate for the interview. Write to them with at least one weeks' notice and explain how the interview will run, what you expect from them and what will happen afterwards. Advise them that they will be asked a mixture of competency based questions and behavioural questions – these will help you to see how they handle and react in different situations.

Ask them to consider a time when they were in a situation; what was it like, how did they behave, what did they do, what did they learn? By talking about something they have experienced, you will get a sense of their emotional response and relate that to how they might deal with similar situations in the future.

For example:

Traditional question: "Have you had experience training new supervisors?"
Improved question: "Tell me about a time when you had to hire and train a new supervisor. How did you go about it? Would you do anything differently?"

There should ideally be two of you in on the interview with one person to record answers and notes, since this helps with the decision making process and reduces bias.

Video interviews: Modern technology means you can interview people anywhere. This is ideal if your candidate doesn't live locally and will save on interview expenses. I would use it as an initial *getting to know you* meeting, and you can use your telephone interview checklist. If they are suitable, then arrange a face–to-face meeting, perhaps alongside a work trial, or spending a day at your office.

Panel interviews: These are often used as a second interview and may include a presentation. These are generally for more senior positions within a business. Give plenty of notice and guidelines if you are asking them to prepare a presentation and advise them who they will be presenting to.

Work trials: A must if you want to see how candidates fit in with your team. Have them spend a day interacting with the team. Ask other team members to get to know the candidates and assess their use of initiative. This can be quite time consuming so I'd perhaps use this when you have whittled down your numbers to two or three applicants. Use an evaluation form and give this to whoever will be supervising your candidates on the day. You could also give a form to anyone else who will interact with your candidates so you are getting a wide range of feedback. I use a "First Impressions" form to gather opinions.

Remember...

Whatever you decide to do, ensure that the candidate is fully aware of the process and the timescales, and anyone else involved in the process is kept informed. How you manage your recruitment and selection process says a lot about you as a business. A poorly managed recruitment campaign will put off candidates and will work against you, especially if they have a few offers to choose from. Put some time aside at the beginning of the process to plan how you are going to interview and select.

Standardise Your Interview Questions

You should always keep any interview notes in a secure manner, as unsuccessful candidates do have the right to request any paperwork relating to their application; the notes should be part of your defence against any claim of discrimination. When taking notes, you should always bear in mind that they will be kept. One HR person was horrified to discover that the only note written down by the interviewer after seeing a candidate was "single mother."

Plan your interview process with consideration.

See appendix 8 for an example of an interview questionnaire.
See appendix 9 for an example of a telephone interview questionnaire.

What type of interviews will you hold? Write down some notes about what you need to do to get the best out of candidates.

_____

_____

_____

_____

_____

_____

_____

_____

_____

_____

_____

_____

_____

_____

_____

_____

Chapter 8
Making Your Decision

"Many managers make poor staffing decisions. By all accounts their batting average is no better than 0.333. At most, one-third of such decisions turn out right; one-third minimally effective; and one-third outright failures. In no other area of management would we put up with such miserable performance." – Peter Drucker, management icon!

How are you going to make your decision on who is the right person for the role?

Consider your evidence
Hold a meeting with the people involved in the interviews and/or the managers they will work for. Review all your evidence.

- CV
- Application form
- Interview form +/- notes
- Work trial feedback
- References

Your decision must be based on the evidence. If someone doesn't feel right after all this time and effort, find evidence to back up your feeling. *Feelings* won't stand up in court if you are challenged on your procedure.

If you are not sure about any of your finalists – start again! Do not take on someone unless you are 100% positive they are right for your business!

References

Most references aren't worth the paper they are written on. Be aware that if you do get a poor reference, it might be sour grapes because they left, or there may have been a personality clash. If you get a similar response from other referees, then you should take them into account when making your decision.

Ask for a reference from their two most recent employers and a character reference. You may have to make the job offer subject to satisfactory references if they don't want you to contact their current employer beforehand.

See appendix 10 for a reference request template.

How to put together a compelling offer

Two to three months are likely to have passed since you first made the decision to hire someone. You have gone through the processes and you are at the final hurdle – the offer.

Remember, while you are putting your candidates through a rigorous selection procedure, they will also be putting you and your business through the same thorough procedure. They must consider whether they really want to work with you or not after all they have witnessed. Start your offer letter by expressing how excited you are to be making this offer. Outline the benefits and salary and make sure that you are offering compensation that reflects the experience and the qualifications of the individual, and also meets their expectations.

What benefits do you offer? Pension? Healthcare? Discounts? Childcare vouchers? Extra holidays? What do your competitors offer? If you can, offer more than they do, such as better shift patterns, opening hours, support network, etc.

Include details of your induction plan so that the applicant is aware of how much thought you have put into their employment, and how much support you are going to provide to ensure they settle in quickly. Finally, it is paramount to make them feel welcome and get them excited enough to accept your offer.

Dealing with rejection

If you are unlucky enough to have your amazing, compelling offer rejected, what are you going to do? Get some feedback on why the candidate said no and revisit each part of the process to see if you could have done anything differently, or improve it for next time. Would any of the other candidates that you took through the whole process be contenders? It's important not to reject the other candidates until you have had an acceptance from your chosen candidate. If none of the other candidates are suitable, it's back to the drawing board!

Choose the right candidate

How do you choose the right candidate? What evidence will you have
gathered?

_____

_____

_____

_____

Respond to all interviewees

What will you offer to your preferred candidate? Write down what's
in your package – salary, holidays, healthcare, pension, etc. How
exciting is your offering?

_____

_____

_____

_____

_____

_____

Chapter 9
The Best Start

There are lots of things you need to consider prior to starting a new employee and there are some things you must have in place by law. You need to:

- Check if they are legally allowed to work in the UK
- Check if you require a criminal record check, or a DBS check if they are working with children?
- Register with HMRC within 4 weeks of starting someone
- Issue a payslip and advise HMRC every time you pay someone
- Be aware of the pension regulations
- Be aware of the minimum wage
- Understand your Health & Safety obligations
- Be aware of their rights to leave for maternity/ paternity/sickness/career breaks/holidays
- Issue them with a written statement of employment particulars within the first two months of their employment.

This statement must include:

- The business's name
- The employee's name, job title or a description of work and start date
- If a previous job counts towards a period of continuous employment, the date the period started
- How much and how often an employee will get paid
- Hours of work, and if employee has to work Sundays, nights or overtime
- Holiday entitlement (and if that includes public holidays)

- Where an employee will be working and whether they might have to relocate
- If an employee works in different places, where these will be and what the employer's address is

You should also include information about:

- How long a temporary job is expected to last
- The end date of a fixed-term contract
- Notice periods
- Collective agreements
- Pensions
- Who to go to with a grievance
- How to complain about how a grievance is handled
- How to complain about a disciplinary or dismissal decision

For up to date employment legislation go to: https://www.gov.uk/browse/employing-people

For Health and Safety updates go to: http://www.hse.gov.uk/getting-started/index.htm

For when it goes wrong: http://www.acas.org.uk/

Most importantly you need to have:

- a compelling vision for the future of your business that gets your new person excited
- a mission statement so your new team member knows how we are going to get there
- a set of values that you and your team live by
- the right culture to foster employee engagement, customer engagement and stakeholder engagement

Induction: Plan a thorough induction programme. It can take new employees on average up to 28 weeks to become fully productive. The more you help them out in the early stage of their employment with you, the quicker they will grasp how you work and start to deliver the results you desire.

Mentor: Identify a mentor – someone who understands the new person's job role and can help them integrate into the team (that might be you if it's your first employee; make time for them!).

Performance Management: Start managing performance from day one. Through the interview process, what areas did you identify that your candidate may need some support or further training with? As part of your induction process, set out your expectations and go through the job description with them. **Agree** on goals for the next year (make sure both of you think these are the right things to do – if your new person is given the freedom to come up with what they think they need to do, they are far more likely to succeed), and break them down into monthly sections. Diarise a monthly one-on-one meeting to go through their progress, provide support, and give positive feedback, as well as pointing out areas for further improvement.

Preparation for induction

Start with a list of everything they need to know from day one. There will be a lot to learn, so you need to prioritise what's urgent and what can wait until later. Be realistic about the time you need to get through all of this. Do not expect them to jump in and be part of the team immediately. Throwing people in at the deep end and seeing if they sink or swim is not useful to anyone.

Think of your new person as a precious seed...

• You know your seed has the ability to grow into something

amazing if the right conditions are provided.

- Give your seed a good quality soil in an appropriate sized container.
- Add in some plant food (it's optional – but you know if it is added in you could get more growth, and faster).
- Place in an area that is sheltered from the elements, but has plenty of sunlight. Check progress every day and regularly top up with fresh water.
- As the seed becomes a seedling, protect from flies and other organisms that might cause harm, and continue nurturing and feeding.
- As the seedling grows and flourishes, ensure that you transfer to a bigger pot when required, so there is always plenty of room for growth and advancement.
- In time you will have a strong, beautiful plant that becomes part of your garden.

If you didn't put the time and effort into your seed, what would happen? It might grow – a little bit. It won't be as strong or as big as it should be, so it won't contribute to the look and feel of your garden in the same way as your nurtured and cared for seed.

Sometimes, despite the best care and nurturing, a seed fails to grow as you had hoped. This is why it may be appropriate to include a probationary period in your contract of employment. This is usually for a three or six-month period, when you can give a new employee one week's notice if things don't work out. Remember though, you and your business are also on a probationary period with your new employee!

What do they need to know?

Design a checklist for your new employee so they see what they are expected to learn.

Once completed, copy and keep with their training records

Who do you involve?

Who should you involve in the induction phase?

There are several elements to the induction and it can be very time consuming for one person. For maximum effectiveness, involve as many people as possible; assign a mentor to oversee the process and to ensure the checklist gets completed.

Have staff with the expertise in each area share their knowledge and use your external stakeholders (customers & suppliers) to give support in what they need from your new employee. The more of your team your new employee can spend time with, the quicker they will build relationships and settle in to the work environment.

At the earlier stage of your company's development you are unlikely to have many employees to help in the induction process, let alone a HR department! In this case, stagger your induction process so it doesn't feel too intense for your new employee, and you can spread the commitment of your precious time.

It is important that you do schedule time for this process, and not be tempted to cancel or put it off until you realise that your new employee has been with you for six months and it's too late!

Week 1:
Once they know where everything is, who everyone is and what's expected of them, have them shadow someone who is doing the same job as they will be expected to do. Even if they come to you with years of experience, you want them to do things your way, from day one.

Week 4:
It's time for a formal review of how the first month has gone. Get

prepared! Look over the objectives that were agreed, make sure their checklist has been completed and review some of their work. Get feedback from their mentor and other stakeholders; ask them for one thing that's gone really well and one thing that could be improved on. Get people used to giving and receiving feedback in this way – it encourages a developmental culture. Give lots of positive feedback and encouragement: are their objectives still relevant; agree on some for the next month; set the date for your next one-on-one. Show your new person that you really care about their involvement in the business and their personal development.

Take Action...
Design a standard induction for your new employees consisting of everything a new person needs to know in order to start working with you. You can add things to it to tailor it specifically to the different roles you recruit for in the future, but have a basic template to get you started.

See appendix 11 for an example induction checklist.

Plan a Thorough Induction

Plan a thorough induction – give your new team member the best start! Make a list of what you need to share with your new employee.

_____

_____

_____

_____

_____

_____

_____

_____

_____

_____

_____

_____

_____

Chapter 10
Performance Management

Performance management should form an integral part of daily working life. We should ALL be always looking to do what we do better, faster and more efficiently.

Day 1 plan for development

During the induction process, draw up a Personal Development Plan or PDP. This outlines the goals you want your new employee to achieve over a period of time, with three to five goals normally being sufficient. These should be SMART goals; SMART is an acronym for:

- **S**pecific – be really specific about **WHAT** you are going to do!
- **M**easure it - how will you know when you have achieved it?
- **A**chievable - can you actually do this yourself, do you have the skills?
- **R**ealistic - is it feasible, does it fit in with your work/life aspirations?
- **T**ime bound - **WHEN** are you going to do it by – set a date for completion.

EG:
S = I am going to design a PDP template today.
M = I will know I have achieved this when I have a usable template.
A = It is achievable as I have done them before; I will design a specific template for the managers to use so we have a standardised process.
R = It is realistic as we have agreed as a business that this is an important part of the performance management process.
T = I can do this today.

Get into the habit of setting your goals using **SMART** as you are much more likely to complete things. Challenge your colleagues to make commitments and get used to being asked yourself, "When will you do that?" when you say you are going to do something.

Put together a folder and keep notes from any meetings you have. If possible, get the employee you have just reviewed to sign the notes at the end of the meeting to say they agree with what was discussed. Re-visit the PDP at each review meeting and in between times if things come up. The PDP should show progress in development and could be used as evidence for performance related bonus schemes. When performance is not going so well, you will have evidence to show that you have identified issues and you have been supporting your employee throughout.

One-on-One

Every month you should carry out a one-on-one review with every team member. The meetings are designed to provide a formal opportunity to *check in* with your team members. The meetings can be as long, or as short as, they need to be – they just need to happen. If time is short, grab five minutes over a coffee. If you put them off, you are sending the message that they are not important and ultimately you don't care about them!

The agenda for the meetings generally should be:

- Update on personal issues (How are things with you?)
- Review of last meeting (What have you achieved this month?)
- Give feedback on positives and any areas for improvement
- Complete a review form and sign off
- Agree a date for your next meeting

Clear enough time in your schedule before each review to look over previous reviews and consider what has come up for them over the last month. Be prepared! Make them informal and friendly. You want to get the best out of people – you do that by building rapport and trust. Have them take responsibility for any actions you agree upon, and to commit to when they will do things by – remember SMART!

Giving feedback is important; your team needs to know when they have done a good job. Equally, you need to tell them when they have not and ensure they are aware of their areas for development! This can be challenging; most of us don't like confrontation. In my experience, the quicker you deal with concerns, the better. If you allow poor performance to go unchecked, you are sending the message that is okay to be sub-standard. Other team members will notice and get frustrated. If this continues, it will become your culture, and you will ruin all the hard work you have put in place.

The important thing to remember about feedback is to focus on the behaviours and actions; refrain from putting the blame onto the employee. When you tell someone that they are bad at something, they have nothing to work on, however, when you tell them what they are doing is bad, they can choose to stop doing that.

There are many ways to give feedback. My favourite is the AID Feedback Model. A stands for actions: what is it that they are doing wrong? I is for Impact: what affect is it having? D is for desired outcome: what do you want them to do instead?

- A = Action - What they are doing well or not so well
- I = Impact - The effect these actions are having
- D = Desired Outcome - How can it be done more effectively?

EG: Sarah is your receptionist. She is bubbly and friendly, and people often comment on how helpful she is. For a few months now she has been really sloppy with time keeping; she is consistently late. She is supposed to start work at 9am, frequently arrives at 9.10/9.15 and last week, arrived at 9.30 twice!

- A = You are consistently late, you are supposed to start work at 9am, you frequently arrive at 9.10/9.15 and last week you arrived at 9.30 on two occasions!
- I = There is no one at the desk to take calls and greet visitors. Your colleagues are having to put off their work to cover the reception desk. If you choose to continue arriving late, you may lose your job.
- D = Aim to arrive at 8.45, so you are ready at your desk in time for the doors opening at 9am.

6 month reviews

This is a good time to do the first formal appraisal and the meeting should last 1 to 2 hours. Give your team member a form to complete in advance of the meeting.

Why are appraisal meetings important?

Appraisals assist your team with performing their jobs to the best of their abilities, maximising job satisfaction and their contribution to the overall objectives for the business. It provides you with the opportunity to focus an individual's performance towards your values and goals.

During the meeting you can follow up on progress with past reviews and identify any training and development needs they have. It provides a structure to review competence in a formal way, and to provide feedback on individual performance.

Preparing for appraisal meetings:

A week or so prior to the meeting, provide an appraisal form to be completed in advance. The completed form should be returned to you in advance of the meeting. Agree on a time and place to hold the meeting and set aside a couple of hours to go out for lunch. Look over past reviews and read over the latest form, then think about what you would like to cover during the meeting.

During the meeting:
This is **your** employee's appraisal and they should be doing most of the talking. Enable your employee to open up and discuss things. Remember, this meeting is all about the employee. You have two ears and one mouth and you should listen and speak in the same ratio!

Discuss what the employee has written, and discuss their skills review. Agree on what areas they need to get further training on.

Agree on goals for the next year **(SMART)** and update their PDP. You should both feel comfortable that what has been discussed and agreed upon is realistic and achievable. Sign the paperwork and finish with setting a date for the next one-on-one review.

After the meeting:
Do what you say you will do and make sure paperwork is completed promptly, if you haven't already completed it during the meeting.

Failing to follow through after an appraisal is a huge disincentive for employees, as it becomes little more than a box-ticking exercise. In one organisation I have come across, members of staff have been known to simply photocopy last year's appraisal form, as nothing has changed in the intervening twelve months.

See appendix 12 for an example appraisal form.
See appendix 13 for an example personal development plan.

Engagement Surveys

My hope is that once you have put everything you have learned from this book in place, this becomes less important. If you have an existing team, and you want to change the culture within your business, this is a great place to start. If you don't have an open culture where your team feels they can approach you, you won't know how your team is feeling and you won't be able to fix things!

There are many ways of getting feedback from your teams – you can simply ask them, have an open forum and discuss the issues. These work well in small teams – providing the leadership team is prepared for some tough feedback about themselves. They don't work so well if the team doesn't feel able to express themselves honestly – this is a problem in itself.

You could use an external company to carry out the survey on your behalf. They will also analyse the results and give you feedback and suggestions on what to do to improve your culture and the engagement of your employees.

You could also design your own online survey using free software such as "Survey Monkey" https://www.surveymonkey.com/ or "Wufoo" http://www.wufoo.com/ . Both are easy to use and they can be anonymous, so the team will hopefully be completely honest. You will then have to do your own analysis.

The most important thing to remember after you have done your survey, give the team feedback on the results and take action to fix the problems.

Take action...
Show your team that you care about them and their contribution to the business. Start managing the performance of your team now. Start with the one-on-ones right away, and keep records!

Manage their performance

Keep your employees engaged and motivated. Write down your process for this, when you will carry out reviews, how often, and what they will include.

_____

_____

_____

_____

_____

_____

_____

_____

_____

_____

_____

_____

_____

About the author

I am a firm but fair leader with the tenacity and determination to get through anything. I have a strong work ethic and I am passionate about enjoying what I do.

With over 25 years of experience in small businesses, I have a great understanding of what businesses need in order to build an engaged, motivated team.

My experience is in HR, Recruitment, Financial Management and Training. My expertise lies within people management, from recruitment to exit. I also enjoy mediation and resolving conflict – the more challenging the better!

I am passionate about employee engagement – we spend a lot of time at work, it should be fun! My mission is to help employers realise that they are the ones who hold the key to creating a happy, fun work environment, full of people who believe in their vision and values, and thrive in a nurturing culture.

Appendices

Appendix 1

Managing Director					
	Finance	HR	Operations (technical specialist)	Marketing	IT
Strategic					
Management					
Day to day					

Appendix 2

	Choose 5 values that are important to you	Why are they important?
1		
2		
3		
4		
5		

Get Out of Your Way™

Appendix 3

JOB DESCRIPTION TEMPLATE

JOB TITLE:

LOCATION:

HOURS OF WORK:

REPORTS TO:

JOB PURPOSE:
SPECIFIC DUTIES AND RESPONSIBILITIES
QUALIFICATIONS & EXPERIENCE
These duties defined in this Job Description are not definitive and may be subject to future amendments following appropriate consultation.

Appendix 4

Person Specification Template

	Essential (must have)	Desirable (nice to have – will train if not)
Skills		
Experience		
Behaviours		

Get Out of Your Way™

Appendix 5

ADVERT TEMPLATE

Business Name:	Location:

About your business:

Describe your business – why is yours a great place to work?

What are the key responsibilities of this role?

What type of person are you looking for?

Values:

Skills:

Qualifications:

Interests:

What are you offering?

Annual Leave:

Bonuses:

CPD:

Healthcare/Sick Pay:

Insurance:

Professional Subscriptions:

Salary:

Advert:

For papers – pull together a summary from the above information – you will probably be restricted by a word limit.

For internet sites – use as much of the above info as you can.

Wendy Sneddon

Appendix 6

TEMPLATE APPLICATION FOR EMPLOYMENT

Please complete the form in black ink and block capitals and return it to *(name)*.

Post applied for: ....

Personal Information

Surname:	
Forenames:	
Title (Mr, Mrs, Miss, etc.):	
Previous names (if any):	
Current address:	
Daytime telephone number:	

Appendix 6 cont'd

Do you have the right to take up employment in the UK? If no, please provide further details.	YES / NO
If you do not have the right to take up employment in the UK, would you wish us to assist you in applying for the right to work?	YES / NO
Dates you are not available for interview	

Education and qualifications

From GCSE or equivalent to degree level in chronological order

Establishment	Qualifications gained

Appendix 6 cont'd

Postgraduate education or study or any other professional qualifications

Establishment	Qualifications gained

Work experience

Please give details of your last three jobs. Any relevant posts held before then may also be mentioned. Please begin with your present or most recent position and then work chronologically backwards.

From	To	Name and address of employer	Job title, description of duties and responsibilities, reason for leaving and salary on leaving

Appendix 6 cont'd

<u>Other Information</u>

Do you have any other training, qualifications, skills or personal qualities relevant to the post (e.g. knowledge of a foreign language, computer literacy, full driving licence, etc.)?

Please give details of, and provide an explanation for, any time when you were not either working or in full-time education.

Have you made a previous application to the company? If so, when was this and what was the outcome?

Please give details of your main extra-curricular activities and interests.

Please use this space to say why you are interested in the post for which you have applied, why you believe you are the best person for the job and provide any other information that may assist your application.

If you are successful, when could you take up your post? How many weeks' or months' notice do you have to give to your current employer?

Wendy Sneddon

Appendix 6 cont'd

If you are disabled, please give details of any special arrangements or adjustments you would require to attend interview.

What are your salary expectations?

Referees

Please give details of two referees, one of whom must be your current or most recent employer, or, if this is an application for your first job, your school teacher or higher/ further education lecturer. Neither referee should be a relative or a contemporary.

First referee	Second referee

Rehabilitation of Offenders Act 1974
In order to protect the public, the post you have applied for is exempt from certain provisions of the Rehabilitation of Offenders Act 1974. You are therefore required to disclose all and any past or pending cautions or convictions, whether spent or otherwise, unless it is either a *protected caution* or a *protected conviction* under the terms of the Rehabilitation of Offenders Act 1974 (Exceptions) Order 1975. All information provided will be kept in the strictest confidence and only used for the purpose of assessing your suitability for the post you have applied for. Please specify below details of all and any past or pending cautions or convictions, whether spent or otherwise, except for protected cautions or convictions. If you have no past or pending cautions or convictions, please specify "None".

Declaration

I declare that the information I have given on this application form is, to the best of my knowledge and belief, true and complete. I understand that if it is subsequently discovered that any statement is false or misleading, or that I have withheld relevant information, my application may be disqualified, or, if I have already been appointed, I may be dismissed.

I hereby consent to the c processing the information supplied on this application form for the purposes of recruitment and selection. I accept that if my application is successful, this application form will form part of my personnel file, and in that case, I consent to the data on it being processed for all purposes in connection with my employment.

Signed: .... Date: ....

Get Out of Your Way™

Appendix 7

APPLICANT SCREENING FORM

JOB: DATE:

Candidate Name ⟶								
CRITERIA								
Experience/Qualifications What do you require?								
Smiley, cheerful, enthusiastic & friendly								
Good organisational skills								
Good at listening								
Ability to remain calm under pressure								
Managing multiple phone calls								
Good oral and written communication skills								
Industry/profession experience								
Customer care								
Sales experience								
Cash handling								
IT literate – word/excel/outlook/internet								
Total Score								

Signed:_____ Date:_____

Appendix 8

Suggested Interview Questionnaire

Complete all sections of this form. The information you provide here will help provide constructive feedback to the candidate and will ensure you have not been discriminative.

Name of Applicant			Locum	Permanent
Venue and Date of interview		Position applied for		
Copy of Identification taken, and signed	Yes No – Reason:			
Standard Questions to ask at interview	Talk me through your CV… What skills and qualities will you bring to our business? Tell me about a time when you delivered quality service; what was that like for you? What responsibilities and achievements have you had to date? How would you handle feedback from a client? Tell me about a time when you had to deal with a difficult client.			

Appendix 8 cont'd

Personality and Fit Section:	Where do you see yourself in 5 years time?	
Motivation/Enthusiasm – *did the candidate show enthusiasm in working for the business – comment*	What are your strongest personal attributes? Where do you see areas for personal growth and self-improvement? Can you tell me about a time when you considered yourself to be a good team player?	
Punctuality – *did the candidate arrive on time for appointment (this could indicate their reliability)*	What interests do you have outside of work? What attracted you to this position?	
Interaction – **How did the candidate interact with other team members?**	Why are you leaving your current position?	
Did the candidate chat to any clients during the interview session? How did this go?		
Did the candidate show interest on what was going on during the session?		
Has the candidate undertaken any CPD recently? What did they learn from this? How did they use it?		
Team members on duty at the time of interview and their feedback		
Action to be taken by:	**Offer:** ... *please confirm start date, salary and hours.*	**Reject:** ... *please provide feedback in below space*

Appendix 9

Suggested Telephone Interview Checklist		Date	

Candidate Details

Applicant Name		PAYE	Company

CONTACT DETAILS

Mobile		Home no	
E-mail address			
Eligible to work in UK?		Visa/Expiry	
Nationality			
What do you know about "business name"?		Little	Moderate	Comprehensive

Type of Work/Availability

Permanent		Locum	
Full- time	Part-time	Availability	
Notice period		Short term	Long term
Dates available			

Current Role

Location		Job Title	
Date From		Date To	

Experience

How many years post qualified experience do you have?		
Do you have any further qualifications?	YES	NO

If yes- details:

Team it/Character

Tell me about a situation at work that didn't go well for you; how did you deal with it?

Tell me about a time when you worked as part of a small team; what was that like?

What are your core values? (What is important to you?) Quality/Responsibility/Integrity/Growth?

What five words would your colleagues/previous colleagues or friends use to describe you?

Describe your strengths

Get Out of Your Way™

Appendix 9 cont'd

Tell me about a time where you had to manage change or new developments at work?

Continual Professional Development (CPD)
What CPD have you undertaken over the last 3 years?

Motivations
What motivated you to apply for this position?
Have you applied or worked for us before?
What are your key strengths?
Have you applied for any other vacancies?
What areas would you like further training in?

Salary	
Current Base Salary	
CPD	
Accommodation	
Transport allowance	
Bonus	

Next stage		
Subject to your application being successful, please provide me with your availability for the next stage, which is a face-to-face interview.		
Day	Date	Time

Notes

Wendy Sneddon

Appendix 10

EMPLOYMENT REFERENCE

Applicant's name: _____

Job title while employed by you: _____

Dates employed with you: _____

Reason for leaving: _____

Summary of job duties whilst employed by you: _____
_____
_____

Please also give your assessment as to the following:

Competence in the job (quality and quantity of work produced):
- ☐ Exceptional
- ☐ Very good
- ☐ Good
- ☐ Above average
- ☐ Satisfactory
- ☐ Below average

Application and attitude to the job and to the company:
- ☐ Exceptional
- ☐ Very good
- ☐ Good
- ☐ Above average
- ☐ Satisfactory
- ☐ Below average

Ability to work without supervision:
- ☐ Exceptional
- ☐ Very good
- ☐ Good
- ☐ Above average
- ☐ Satisfactory
- ☐ Below average

Ability to manage workload and work under pressure:
- ☐ Exceptional
- ☐ Very good
- ☐ Good
- ☐ Above average
- ☐ Satisfactory
- ☐ Below average

Honesty and trustworthiness:
- ☐ Exceptional
- ☐ Very good
- ☐ Good
- ☐ Above average
- ☐ Satisfactory
- ☐ Below average

Appendix 10 cont'd

Timekeeping record:
- ☐ Exceptional
- ☐ Very good
- ☐ Good
- ☐ Above average
- ☐ Satisfactory
- ☐ Below average

Relations with other work colleagues:
- ☐ Exceptional
- ☐ Very good
- ☐ Good
- ☐ Above average
- ☐ Satisfactory
- ☐ Below average

Relations with clients, customers and suppliers:
- ☐ Exceptional
- ☐ Very good
- ☐ Good
- ☐ Above average
- ☐ Satisfactory
- ☐ Below average

Does the applicant have a current disciplinary or performance review record?   YES / NO
If yes, please specify the level of warning given, relevant date and a summary of the offence committed/performance issues:

Were there any disciplinary or performance allegations or issues outstanding that had not been investigated or brought before a formal disciplinary or performance management hearing before the termination of the applicant's employment, or which only came to light after the applicant had left employment?   YES / NO
If yes, please provide a summary of the alleged disciplinary or performance issues and provide any other relevant information:

Any other comments:

Would you re-employ this person?   YES / NO
If no, why not?

Signed:

Name:

Position:

Date:

Wendy Sneddon

Appendix 11

Induction Form

Name _____   **Start Date**_____

	Date	Initials

Mentor assigned _____ _____

New Starter Form returned *(Do you have all their details?)* _____ _____

Contract signed and filed *(This is a legal requirement)* _____ _____

Read Team Handbook (If you don't have one – you should) _____ _____

Health and safety manual (Show where it's kept, set timescales for reading through, highlight responsibilities and the policy) _____ _____

Medical Form returned (if you take on someone with past medical issues, _____ _____ they should state if, and how, they may affect their ability to do their job, and what you need to do to provide support)

P45 received _____ _____

Copy of driving licence received (If required) _____ _____

Copy of passport received (you need to know they have permission to work in the UK) _____ _____

Work Permit received (if applicable) _____ _____

Uniform, name badge, keys etc. _____ _____

Introduction to other team members _____ _____

Premises tour including team facilities, fire exits and first aider _____ _____

Introduction to the business, vision, mission, values and culture _____ _____

Familiarised with Absence/Holiday Request Procedure _____ _____

Computer training _____ _____

Product, service & marketing training (What do they need to know about _____ _____ what you do?)

Personal development plan (PDP) agreed _____ _____

One-on-one meetings booked into the diary _____ _____

Signed by Employee_____   **Signed by Line Manager**_____
Once completed, copy and keep with their training records

Get Out of Your Way™

Appendix 12

Example Appraisal

Name:	Date:
What has gone well with your performance?	
What hasn't gone well with regard to your performance?	
What will you do differently to improve this?	
How can we support you?	
What else would you like to discuss during your appraisal?	
Managers Comments:	
Employees signature:	Managers signature:

Appendix 13

Personal Development Plan

What are my development objectives?	What activities do I need to undertake to achieve my objectives?	What support/resources do I need to achieve my objectives	Target date for achieving	Actual date of achieving

Review Date:
Comments:

Made in the USA
Lexington, KY
10 March 2018